*To Jennifer,
Betty S.
I hope you enjoy this book.
Joyce*

SUNNY THOUGHTS
For Cloudy Days

PAUSE
PONDER
PRAY
PRAISE

BETTY SMITH

Copyright © 2014 Betty Smith. All Rights Reserved.

All Scripture quotations, unless otherwise indicated, are taken from the *Holy Bible, New International Version*®. *NIV*®. Copyright © 1973, 1978, 1984 by International Bible Society. Used by permission of Zondervan. All rights reserved.

Book Design and Production by WatersDesigns.com

ISBN: 978-0-9883279-6-2

Library of Congress Control Number: 2014937330

First Edition: April 2014

Please visit the author's web site at:
www.BettyWSmith.com

Printed in the USA

Acknowledgments

My special thanks to:

Shari Waters for her expertise and technical support.

Sandra Ray for being an excellent and tactful editor.

Sharon Fleming for critiquing the manuscript and offering invaluable suggestions.

Margaret Newberry for reading the manuscript and giving me good advice.

Ann Cobb for her encouragement and guidance without whom this book would not have been possible. She is also the author of the four P's (Pause, Ponder, Pray, and Praise) on the cover.

I humbly dedicate this book to:

The glory of God, as He continues to amaze me daily with His power and love.

The memory of my husband, George, for his strength of character and love for his family.

My children, Vicki and Phil, Pat and Clark, Tommy, Keith and Karen, who continue to make me proud.

My grandchildren and great-grandchildren, who light up my life and keep me young at heart.

Table of Contents

Introduction 7
A Cup of Cold Water 9
Are You Really Tuned In? 11
Attitude Pills 15
Be Happy? 17
The Best of Times, The Worst of Times 19
Building Good Memories 23
Checking My Bucket List 25
Childlike Faith 27
Choices 29
Courtesies are Priceless 31
Dangers of Instant Gratification 33
Dealing with Interruptions 35
Do You Carry a Hat Pin? 39
Do You Need Recalibrating? 43
Equipped for Service 45
Eyes for the Big Picture 47
Friendship 49
Games People Play 51
Gathering Feathers Is No Fun 53
Gifts That Keep on Giving 55
Grandparents Are a Different Breed 57
Holding Fast to the Rock 61
How Does Adversity Affect You? 63
How Important Are Our Gifts? 67

If You Don't Use It, You Lose It 71
I'm Sorry 73
In the Twinkling of an Eye 77
Is Busyness Your Idol? 79
It's Not My Fault 81
Joy of Ordinary Days 85
Laughter is Good Medicine 87
When Life Tosses You a Lemon, Make Lemonade 89
Living in the Shadow of Fear 91
Need a Memory Pill? 93
Music, the Universal Language 95
Relinquishing Control 97
Sanding the Rough Edges 99
Seasons of Change 101
Seeing is Believing — Or Is It? 103
Sitting on the Fence 105
Squandering Your Inheritance 107
Teach Them to Love 109
The Gift of Life 111
The Other Side of the Mountain 113
The Power of the Tongue 115
Time Is a Very Special Gift 117
What Difference Can One Person Make? 119
When All Else Fails, Read the Instructions 121
Why Pray? 123
Your Beans Always Come Up 125

Introduction

This book is a compilation of lighthearted devotional thoughts written to give encouragement for the present and hope for the future. It is my sincere prayer that these simple words will bring glory to God and a ray of sunshine to each reader.

Some portions of these writings have been published over the past several years in *The News and Farmer/The Jefferson Reporter*, the local newspaper in Louisville, Georgia.

A Cup of Cold Water

"I tell you the truth, anyone who gives you a cup of water in my name because you belong to Christ will certainly not lose his reward."
MARK 9:41

On one of summer's hottest days, I attended the graveside funeral of a relative at a small country church. Afterward, many of us were visiting under the shade of a graceful old oak tree, reliving our childhood memories. The perspiration and gnats were seriously interfering with our fellowship when out of the blue someone came out with an ice chest filled with bottled water. What a brilliant gesture. It was as refreshing as an oasis in the middle of a desert.

At another time, as skies were gray and our outlook daunted, an old friend rang the doorbell, and his short visit lifted our spirit beyond words. God uses people every day to minister in His name. Generally, we are unaware of the impact that such a simple deed as making a phone call, dropping by for a visit, or offering a cup of cold water may have on the recipient.

Some people seem to be especially attuned to opportunities like these. They have the knack for knowing just what to do and when to do it. God gives each of us opportunities for service. Our roles may be those of encouraging, listening, having sympathetic hearts, or meeting physical needs as simple as a cup of cold water on a hot day.

The Bible teaches that little things do mean a lot. There is the story of the lad who brought his lunch of five loaves and two fishes to be blessed by the Savior, and He used it to feed over five thousand. Then there is the story of the widow's mite. Her gift has been used as an example of love and generosity for God and His church over the centuries and has inspired other contributions of immeasurable value. God's emphasis is not on the cost of the gift or time involved in the giving. It is on the gift itself and the spirit with which it is given. These examples show what God can accomplish through our simplest gestures when they are dedicated to His service.

Are You Really Tuned In?

"He who has ears, let him hear."
MATTHEW 11:15

My ten-year-old grandson and I were discussing the necessity of *really listening*, using the two ears, one mouth illustration. During our conversation, it was evident that his mind was out in left field, and my own words reminded me that I have been guilty of not listening myself.

Being able to sincerely listen is exceedingly important. Words may enter our ear canal and be interpreted by our brain then quickly move out the other ear, never to be thought of again. This is not only true of young children and teens but also of adults of all ages. How long has it been since you were discussing something of importance with your spouse only to realize he or she was not tuned in to your station? You may have experienced this same response while presenting a concern to your superior at work or a friend with whom you wish to confide. It's frustrating not to be heard and understood.

Relationships are inhibited, dreams are thwarted, and discouragement may abound.

Surely no one intends to be insensitive by not listening, so why do we not hear? The reasons are numerous. Children may be thinking of the next video game they will play. Or it may be a fast-moving, action-packed movie that consumes their thinking. Teen priorities are of a different nature but may not include a mind open to advice and direction. Then, for adults, who should know better, it may be their work, their hobby, or their pursuit of success and/or wealth, none of which will be important without family and meaningful relationships.

God must become most frustrated of all as He tries to communicate with us only to find that we are not really tuned in to His message. We may read our Bible, attend church, and even pray, but is it a one-sided conversation? Is it all geared to our wish list and not His?

His directive to his followers two thousand years ago is the same to us today. In *The Message*, a contemporary translation of the Bible, Matthew 11:15 reads this way: *Are you listening to me? Really listening?* We can be sure that when the LORD, who spoke the universe into being, speaks to us, we would do well to listen.

Attitude Pills

Your attitude should be the same as that of Christ Jesus: . . . he humbled himself and became obedient to death—even death on a cross!
PHILIPPIANS 2:5,8B

In our day of modern medicine, with drugs to treat so many health problems, isn't it a shame that we don't have an attitude pill? Don't you know people to whom you'd like to give a truckload? As a matter of fact, most of us could use some for ourselves.

I can think of a number of people, including me, who could benefit from such a pill at times. Some are *pessimists*. You know the ones I mean—the people who are never glad about anything. They expect the worst from people and usually get it. They seem to enjoy being miserable and want to make sure that everyone else is in the same boat. Then there are the *faultfinders*. They spend ten times more energy and thought enumerating the things that are wrong in the world than considering what they might do to make improvements. They are also the ones who consider themselves victims of every circumstance and refuse to accept responsibility for anything. Whatever happens is someone else's fault. *Know-it-alls* might benefit from these pills from time to time just to give them a taste of humility, and *bullies* could use a role reversal experience, just to get a new perspective. *Monday-morning quarterbacks* might also profit from doses on occasion to remind them that everyone has 20/20 hindsight.

A touch of one or all of the above attitudes may surface in everyone occasionally, but they do not need to become a habit.

Jesus has set the tone for our approach to life. Regardless of our circumstances, He made it possible for us to live with hope, not despair, with a spirit of triumph, not defeat, with love for the unlovely, and faith in the unseen. Armed with His message, our attitudes can reflect joy and peace. It's true, we don't have a pill to prescribe, but we do have a message to share, and what a powerful message it is!

Be Happy?

To the man who pleases him, God gives wisdom, knowledge and happiness...
ECCLESIASTES 2:26

If you are a parent, chances are you have said to your child at least once, "My wish for you is to be happy." I know I have. Thinking back, I never remember my mother having said that to me. Things she did say were golden goodies like "A good name is rather to be chosen than silver or gold;" "Pretty is as pretty does;" and "Treat others as you want to be treated." She was a wise lady and knew fully well that genuine happiness is not a goal to be sought but a by-product of doing God's will.

Somewhere between then and now, change has taken place in our society. The focus seems to be geared more toward giving children more *things* and sparing them the burden of hard work and sacrifice. Part of this is attributable to all the work-saving devices we have that our parents did not enjoy and the fact that there are fewer chores to do. However, being happy for most people means getting what they want, when they want it, by attempting to satisfy every desire. We can see the results of this kind of life by looking at the parable of the prodigal son (Luke 15:11-32). In the end he was anything but happy. Most of us have ventured into that foreign country at some time in our lives only to find disappointment and heartbreak.

What then should we pursue in life? Jesus tells us in Matthew 6:33, "But seek first his kingdom and his righteousness, and all these things will be given to you as well." God has clearly given us directives for living the abundant life in His Word. He has not given these directives to deprive us of having fun but rather to spare us the horrible consequences of becoming a slave to our own selfish desires.

What a blessing it is for young people to know and heed these instructions early in life. Still, it is never too late to begin. God stands with open arms to receive us, battle scars and all!

The Best of Times, The Worst of Times

Give thanks to the LORD, for he is good; his love endures forever.
PSALM 118:29

We can celebrate the goodness of God in every era of life. Each one brings joys and challenges. At least, I have found it to be so. The beginning of *A Tale of Two Cities*, "It was the best of times, it was the worst of times…" could very well be used to describe every age.

The wonderful teen years are so exciting. Every new relationship brings with it a sense of enthusiasm so real it is hard to contain. Every decision is intense, and because it is, any glitch in plans is a major catastrophe. Teenagers face the challenge of school, decisions about college, and keeping a sense of balance between responsibility and joyful exuberance.

The era of decision-making about a career, a mate, when to have a family, where to live, and so on, brings with it a different set of pleasures and concerns. Each step seems more critical than the last.

The rearing-of-children period is an education in itself and brings with it responsibilities as well as a new appreciation for God's precious gifts. However, the pace continues to mount, and it is easy to become overwhelmed with the work involved and miss some of the priceless moments.

The empty-nest syndrome comes next. Now, the children you urged to study and become self-sufficient, do so, and you are crying because they are no longer at home. That period also has its benefits. There is peace and quiet to do some things you haven't had time to do for yourself. However, by now, you may have forgotten what it was that you wanted to do.

Soon grandchildren come into the picture. You can love them, spoil them, and take them home when you're tired. You hardly notice that your joints are getting stiffer, and you don't move as swiftly anymore.

The "golden years" follow and have been described as times when it takes a lot of gold for health maintenance and joint repairs. Thank the Lord for replacement parts.

So whether it is the best of times or the worst of times in your life right now, you can know that God is at work weaving His pattern of perfection.

Building Good Memories

Remember your Creator in the days of your youth, before the days of trouble come and the years approach when you will say, "I find no pleasure in them."
ECCLESIASTES 12:1

One of the treasures of the golden years is reliving the memories of your youth. It is, therefore, imperative to build good memories! The writer of Ecclesiastes makes the point that it is important to honor God when you are young. *The Message* (a modern translation of Ecclesiastes 12:1) puts it this way:

> *Honor and enjoy your Creator while you're still young,*
>
> *Before the years take their toll and your vigor wanes,*
>
> *Before your vision dims and the world blurs,*
>
> *And the winter years keep you close to the fire.*

It may be hard for young parents, with so many demands in their lives, to imagine how precious those memories will be or how important these years are in the life of their children. God doesn't give anyone a more important responsibility than being a Christian parent. Soon, you will look back and wonder where the time went.

Then, your heart will swell with pride and thanksgiving as you witness your children become responsible adults.

It is not only important to build good memories but to record and preserve them as well. How I regret not having kept a journal of events in the life of our family. There are so many dates that have become blurred and some forgotten. Still, there are enough left to cherish and brighten my life forever.

God's blessings are new every morning and are as numerous as the stars. Memories are just a few of them. However, we still need to be reminded that, regardless of our age, our focus should not be on the past, because the best is *always* yet to come.

Checking My Bucket List

Each man's life is but a breath.
PSALM 39:5B

News alert! Days are no longer made up of twenty-four hours! In the twinkling of an eye, one day merges into the next and goes by more quickly than the one before. Such is the status for seniors. Birthdays are monthly, or so they seem, and there is a feeling of urgency to live life to the fullest. The faster the merry-go-round, the fewer things get checked off my bucket list.

One of my biggest challenges is adjusting to change, a skill I once handled with ease. Just when life is racing at the speed of light, my body is gearing down and marching to a different drummer. There is a longing to spend more time savoring morning coffee and watching the beautiful redbird outside my window instead of rushing to get "things" done. Rushing is a thief that robs us of appreciation of simple things and the joys they bring. Been there, done that!

This electronic age is also a challenge. I am computer literate but still struggle with using three or four remotes to retrieve movies through Xbox and Netflix or stream through the Internet.

If you have outlived your former pastor, you may have noticed a change in the order of your worship service or the music at your church. Yes, even churches are changing. Many have adapted to a broader spectrum of music and messages to try and accommodate the preferences of congregations of all age groups. Even so, it is very difficult to please everyone with anything. The important thing is that God's truths do not change. In fact, I doubt that He is the least bit concerned with the order of service or the type of music if it is done "in spirit and in truth." We are the ones who sweat the small stuff.

I must admit being a senior is not all bad. It certainly beats the alternative. Understanding and hope that come from experiencing God's power and wisdom over the years are priceless. Each day becomes more precious, and the assurance that the best is yet to come puts the icing on the cake!

Childlike Faith

And he said: "I tell you the truth, unless you change and become like little children, you will never enter the kingdom of heaven. Therefore, whoever humbles himself like this child is the greatest in the kingdom of heaven."
MATTHEW 18:3-4

Gary shuddered as his father told him they would be leaving in a few minutes to go to the dentist. He remembered his visit the previous week when the dentist told his mother he had a small cavity that needed to be filled. The dentist explained the procedure and showed him the instruments that he would use. Gary remembered how gross they looked, and fear gripped his whole body. How could the week have passed so quickly, and why was his dad taking him instead of his mom? Was it going to be that dreadful?

Gary's dad could see the fear in his son's eyes and began to reassure him that even though it might hurt a little, it would be good for him in the end. "Son, I can promise you that a little pain now is better than to lose a tooth. I will be with you and you will be fine." To Gary, that sounded a lot like what his mom had said to him the last time she carried him to the doctor for an immunization. *How can anything so painful and scary be good for me?* he thought.

Gary did not understand the necessity of a filling, but one thing he did know. His dad and mom loved him very much, and he did not believe they would allow him to hurt without a purpose. With this in mind he was able to endure the procedure with a minimum of stress. It was a matter of trust.

Most of us have suffered many things in life more painful than a filling and have experienced God's presence with us at those times. Even so, we still are not exempt from the feelings of apprehension and fear and times of uncertainty. The ability to trust completely is an ongoing learning experience which won't be totally completed until we're taken home. Still, we can learn from Gary, in his simple faith, because we know our Father, and we know He loves us. Knowing this does not take away the pain, but it gives us strength to endure.

Choices

May the God of hope fill you with all joy and peace as you trust in him, so that you may overflow with hope by the power of the Holy Spirit.
ROMANS 15:13

Many people find themselves in a dilemma of despair because of bad choices they have made and as a result spend much of the remainder of their lives with regret. This is genuinely sad and a reminder that our choices affect our lives. The argument can be made that life is a series of circumstances beyond our control. Some proponents of this line of thought are content to sit back and place blame. Many circumstances really are beyond our control. Yet, ultimately the choices we make in spite of, or in response to, situations are what make us winners or losers.

Regardless of our circumstances, I believe we are responsible for decisions we make, or fail to make, and everyone makes wrong ones at times. Even then, every new day brings new opportunities. We have to determine whether we will whine about the wrong choices, or learn from them, put them behind us, and forge ahead. That is an ongoing challenge.

Fear of making wrong choices causes some not to make any choice at all. Still, a decision is made, even if it is one not to decide. Sometimes it is easier to play Scarlet O'Hara and say, "I'll think about that tomorrow." When tomorrow comes, the problem still remains and may have become even more difficult to solve. The procrastinator may suffer from lost opportunities and regrets. In fact, most difficulties do not go away when ignored. While lost opportunities or wrong choices can never be recovered or changed, they can be forgiven and life goes on.

Our challenge is to strive to use wise judgment, keep a hopeful attitude, and focus on seeing our glass as half full rather than half empty. If it is half full, our challenge is to continue to fill it to the brim. If it is half empty, our challenge is the same.

God's Word promises that He will never leave us, and as we look to Him, we can have hope for the future, whatever our circumstances. A lot depends upon our making the right choices, beginning today.

Courtesies are Priceless

"Do to others as you would have them do to you."
LUKE 6:31

Do you ever get the feeling that little courtesies like *please* and *thank you* have fallen by the wayside? It is possible to spend a whole day in today's world without receiving a single kind word. Certainly, we expect to get them at home, but what about those people who live alone? If they don't get encouragement and niceties from outside contacts, they don't get any.

I am especially reminded of the importance of nice manners and appreciative attitudes when I shop and the salesperson acts like he or she enjoys giving good service or when a delivery person exhibits enthusiasm and a big smile. Just a simple smile and thank you makes one's day more pleasant. Children who have been taught courtesies and respect for others have been given a treasure that will bring them rich rewards.

Communication is so important. Unless we intend to live in a bubble, we need to understand how much we are missing if we do not exhibit a courteous, considerate attitude toward others. If you are a "What's in it for me?" kind of person, you may be shocked to learn that you are missing many kind responses and possibly loyal friends by your curt and callous attitude.

We are known by the messages we send through our actions and words. Yes, communication includes body language and attitudes. Every word that comes from our mouth and every act of kindness, or lack thereof, paint one more stroke on the portrait of us that others see. Why, then, would one not realize how essential it is to build kindness and consideration into daily living?

The Golden Rule is not just a cliché. It is a basic principle of the good life that Jesus intended for us to enjoy. A good place to start is at home. Remember to say thank you to your spouse for the little things he or she may do for you. Find things for which to praise your children. Their responses may surprise you. And for goodness sake, smile and be courteous to your daily contacts outside the home. Your smile may be the only one they get all day!

Dangers of Instant Gratification

Once when Jacob was cooking some lentil stew, Esau came in from the open country, famished. He said to Jacob, "Quick, let me have some of that red stew! I'm famished!" Jacob replied, "First sell me your birthright." "Look, I am about to die," Esau said. "What good is the birthright to me?" (So he sold his birthright to Jacob.)
GENESIS 25:29-34

The older I get, the more difficult it becomes to curb my appetite and manage my weight. It is clear that even in this late stage of my life, self-discipline concerning food is still a big problem.

I remember having been taught the story of Jacob and Esau as a young person, how Esau sold his birthright for a bowl of lentil stew, and wondering, *How can anyone have been so weak?* Now I know! Evidently, Esau loved food as much as I do, and in a fit of hunger, was willing to forfeit his father's and God's rich blessings for his life for one short period of gratification. What a waste!

We live in an age of instant gratification for all sorts of things, be it food, sex, material possessions, power, or fame. More often than not, we sell ourselves far short of

God's intended blessings because of our "gotta have it now" mentality. Ever wondered what valuable things you may have forfeited because of disobedience or rash decisions? The good news is we don't have to continue. It is never too late for a new start. God can help us see things from His perspective and decipher what is best for the long haul.

Prayer: Lord, give me the grace to control my appetite for instant gratification for worldly things, including food, knowing that your plan is perfect and leads to genuine abundant life.

Dealing with Interruptions

"I tell you, get up, take your mat and go home."
MARK 2:11

I often find myself evaluating achievements of the day. This is necessary for me, or else the days fly by and my to-do list remains unchanged. It occurred to me recently that what really may need evaluating is the unit of measure I am using. A successful day cannot be evaluated by a list. It might be more appropriate to determine how the interruptions and opportunities were taken in stride and used to the maximum. I find myself longing for a day with no disruptions but often discover those days are my least productive times. It only takes a quick look at how Jesus handled the unexpected to get my priorities back on track.

One of the Bible stories that was etched in my mind as a child was the one in Mark 2:1-12. I can still see the big picture on our Sunday school room wall. There were four men on a flat roof of a stucco house. They were lowering a paralytic on a stretcher through a hole they had made in the roof. It was the only way they could get their friend in to see Jesus because of the huge crowd gathered there. Jesus was in a house in Capernaum. The crowd was so great, many could not get in. The doorways were blocked and people spilled over outside. Jesus was inside teaching when he heard noises on the roof and pieces of clay and dust began to fall on them. Soon he was able to see the face of someone peeping through the hole, and finally a type of stretcher was lowered carrying the paralytic. Think of it. What a disruption! What a mess it had made in the house. Instead of being agitated or thrown off track, Jesus looked upon the man with compassion and was impressed by the faith of his friends. He stopped what he was doing and took the opportunity to heal the paralytic. He began by healing him spiritually through forgiveness of sins and then physically by saying, "I tell you, get up, take your mat and go home" (Mark 2:11).

Instead of becoming irate because of the messy and abrupt entrance, Jesus saw men of great faith and determination. He saw men so concerned about a disabled friend they were willing to risk humiliation and reprimand to bring him to Jesus.

What an example He set for us. I believe one truth Jesus might have us learn from this passage is not to get upset about the unexpected events that come to all of us. They may be some of the most important opportunities for service we ever have!

Do You Carry a Hat Pin?

And let us consider how we may spur one another on toward love and good deeds.
HEBREWS 10:24

It has been said there are three categories of people: those who watch things happen, those who make things happen, and those who don't know what's happening. I submit to you that there are two other groups that may be added to the three above. My guess is you know some of these people.

Imagine yourself ready to embark on a new job with all the enthusiasm you can muster. It will require many changes in your life including relocation. Your confidence level is high, and you feel good about the decision you have made. You call a friend to share your good news only to have him throw a wet blanket of pessimism over you like a black cloud. Your friend responds with comments such as "You're going to hate that area. You realize the crime rate is extremely high." Or "I turned down that job last year, but I'm sure you'll like it." Or "You realize there's no future in that kind of work!" These comments rekindle all the fears through which you've struggled in making your decision, and your enthusiasm fades as quickly as air escapes from a simple prick in a balloon. It seems as though some people walk around on a daily basis with a hat pin looking for balloons to stab!

Then there are encouragers. They seem to know just the right things to say to make things seem better. Encouragers accept you at face value and have faith in your ability even when you've lost it in yourself. They promote confidence with their knack for lifting your spirits and dispelling fear and timidity. In contrast, people with hat pins seem to delight in deflating hopes, dreams, confidence, and joy.

What makes these two groups so different in their approach to life? I have no qualifications to make a diagnosis, but my ventured guess would be linked to their relationship with God. It is only when we have hope in our own hearts that we are able to pass it on to others, and without God, there is no hope.

It is my prayer that the number of encouragers will increase and the hat pin carriers will trade their hat pins for pumps.

Do You Need Recalibrating?

Search me, O God, and know my heart; test me and know my anxious thoughts. See if there is any offensive way in me, and lead me in the way everlasting.
PSALM 139:23-24

Recently, it came to my attention that my piano needed tuning. It's amazing that an instrument without much use can become out of tune just sitting there. All musical instruments fall into this category. In contemplating this phenomenon, my thoughts focused on other similar situations. Consider scales. In order for them to be deemed accurate, they must be calibrated on a regular basis. In fact, instruments of all descriptions require calibration or tuning. The more precise the accuracy required, the more frequent the calibration needed.

If inanimate objects must be in tune for good performance, how much more important is it that our minds and hearts be in tune with our Creator? Left unto ourselves, we can easily drift off course without even realizing it. Just as when two points separate slightly at first, the farther each goes in its own direction, the farther apart they become, so go our lives as we drift.

As a youngster, the beach was my favorite place to visit. It was such fun to get on a raft and drift out and ride the waves back in to shore. Much to the horror of my parents, I failed to see the danger of drifting out too far.

Life can be like that! God has made provisions to prevent us from drifting and means by which we can recalibrate our lives. It does require action on our part. He has given us a book of instructions. He has given us the perfect example to follow and His Holy Spirit for our guide. As we look up and our eyes meet His, our lives are brought into perspective with the perfect pattern. At that moment, our imperfections are made plain. His hand reaches out to us, and as we submit to His perfect will, He begins the process of making us just like His perfect pattern. Being made into a new creation can be painful. It may require the total transformation of our lifestyle. However, we can be assured that what God has in mind for us will lead to ultimate peace, joy, and perfection in the end!

Equipped for Service

*...the earth is full of your creatures.
These all look to you to give them their food at the
proper time.*
PSALM 104:24, 27

It fascinates me that some animals and birds can be trained to follow instructions and communicate with human beings. The fascination is twofold: (1) that the creatures can be taught without speaking our language; (2) that there are people with the patience and know-how to teach them. I recently witnessed a "birds of prey" show in which a bald eagle, a hawk, and a falcon were the stars. Their wingspans were accentuated as they soared with great speed and in exceedingly close proximity to our heads. We could have easily reached up and touched them, except for the warning that fingers might be mistaken for chicken pieces.

Each bird had its own distinctive characteristics and remarkable skills. My grandson and I were reminded once again of the Creator's awesome power. We were told that birds of prey have extremely good eyesight and astounding strength in their feet and that some can move with speed approaching two hundred miles per hour. But listen to this! They see things *faster* than we do. This vision is necessary to spot speeding targets of food for the next meal. Now seeing better, more clearly, farther, or more definitively is easy to understand, but faster takes a little thought. The explanation was given that the fast-moving frames in video games, action movies, and even commercials would be considered slow moving and very boring to those birds. Wow!

The area was serene with breathtaking scenery and the show was entertaining, but the most important lesson to be remembered for me was the sufficiency of God's grace. He provides the skills those birds need to survive. Contrary to what chicken farmers may think, the birds' role is important in the scheme of God's creation. If He equips the birds for their survival, how much more does He equip us to fulfill His purpose in our own lives?

If you have the inclination, do a little research on birds of prey. Another humbling fact to keep in mind is that no matter how technically advanced our world may become, God was here first. His creations are truly awesome!

Eyes for the Big Picture

"Blessed is the king who comes in the name of the Lord! Peace in heaven and glory in the highest!"
LUKE 19:38

If you want to see how quickly public opinion can change, you need look no further than Palm Sunday in the life of Jesus. Just days before His crucifixion, the Bible paints a vivid picture of throngs of followers strewing palm branches in His path as He traveled His final journey to Jerusalem (Luke 19:28-38). You can feel the excitement of His followers as they sang praises to the long-awaited Messiah! They had yearned for His coming. The Jewish nation would no longer be subservient to Roman rule. Freedom would be theirs at last!

Little did they know that in just days their dreams would be shattered. Instead of singing praises to the Messiah, they would be engulfed in a crowd shouting, "Crucify him!" (Luke 23:21).

Since we are on the other side of the cross, it is easy for us to recognize that the followers of Jesus had completely misunderstood His mission. Their hearts were longing for relief from the "here and now" without a notion of the big, timeless picture. Therefore, rather than standing in support of the man whom they had seen heal the sick and raise the dead, they were swallowed up in fear and confusion and ran away.

If we examine the circumstances closely, we may be able to identify some of our own traits in these frightened followers. Remember how, in the throws of agony, we may have prayed for immediate relief for the healing of a loved one or restoration of a relationship? Our answer may have been quite different from our request. As a result, the inclination may have been to run away in frustration and disbelief. But, when the morning comes, as it always does, God ministers to our broken hearts and brings His peace in proportion to our trust.

We can be thankful God does not answer all our prayers in the way we ask. In the scheme of the big picture, we can know He always has something more wonderful in store for us and our loved ones than we could imagine or ask. We may not ever fully understand His plan on this side of heaven, but we can know His love and peace and that His grace is sufficient.

Friendship

"Greater love has no one than this, that he lay down his life for his friends. You are my friends if you do what I command."
JOHN 15:13-14

MasterCard has a commercial that reminds us of the value of certain experiences in life that cannot be bought. They may range from things as simple as a smile on a child's face to the beauty of a mountain range. I think you'll agree that many of life's treasured moments are priceless. I also believe you'll agree that friends are cherished gifts from God.

Friends are ones who know us well and love us anyway. They are slow to anger, slow to judge, and quick to respond when we are in trouble. They can detect weariness in our eyes or a gleam in our heart. They know when to talk and when to listen, when to stay and when to go. They can rejoice with us without being envious and grieve with us as though they have been smitten in our stead.

Friends cannot be bought, borrowed, or given away. They stand by us in the face of adversity and stand up for us in time of criticism. They overlook our shortcomings and praise our strengths. They speak the truth, even when we may fail to appreciate it, and they always have our best interest at heart.

Friends are not self-centered, jealous, hypocritical, or vindictive. Instead, they are kind, caring, thoughtful, optimistic, and true. They are available, regardless of their own busy schedule, and can be relied upon to keep everything in strictest confidence. If you have one such person in your life, consider yourself rich beyond measure. God, in His infinite wisdom, often chooses to minister to us through other people. Friends are some of His chosen vessels. In fact, in John 15:13-14, Jesus depicts friendship at its highest level.

God has blessed every believer with a measure of spiritual gifts dedicated to His service. Surely, being equipped to be a true friend is one of those gifts. Jesus set the example and called us to follow in His steps. What is a better way to glorify the Savior than to demonstrate his example of true friendship to others?

Games People Play

Do not cast me away when I am old; do not forsake me when my strength is gone.
PSALM 71:9

A trip to the grocery store can be an adventure. In addition to buying food, it's a place to socialize, to catch up on the news, and to play guessing games. Guessing games go like this. You meet a familiar person, she begins a conversation, as if she is your long lost friend—and you cannot remember her name. You know her well, but you are drawing a blank, and it's too embarrassing to confess. The only sensible thing to do is to continue your conversation, hoping she will give you a clue to jog your memory. Sometimes she will, and you're off the hook. Sometimes she doesn't, and you leave bewildered, asking the next person you meet, "What is that lady's name?"

Taking relatives and friends to church can be even more challenging for me since I am expected to introduce them to everyone. Now I see this same congregation every Sunday, and some are close friends. But for some unknown reason, I may not recall their names quickly. I have a mental block that borders on idiocy when it comes to names. If, by chance, any of you can identify with this syndrome, let me suggest a remedy. You can either make a quick retreat to the restroom or sing in the choir and let the guests fend for themselves.

Another game that is quite a challenge is called "Why am I here?" It goes like this. A simple trip outside to pick up the morning paper can result in picking up litter, getting mail from the mailbox left from yesterday, and complete amnesia causing me to wonder, *Why did I come outside?* That concept applies to inside as well as I waste time going from room to room to do something important, I'm sure.

I don't think I have Alzheimer's, so my only other conclusion is that brains are like computers and mine definitely needs updating. That leaves me with but one alternative—to be content that I can eventually remember names, be thankful for every day, and enjoy the games we play until my updated brain is ready in heaven. What a marvelous hope God has given those who trust Him.

Gathering Feathers Is No Fun

"But I tell you that men will have to give account on the day of judgment for every careless word they have spoken. For by your words you will be acquitted, and by your words you will be condemned."
MATTHEW 12:36-37

One of the things I like about writing is having the opportunity to reread and think about what I have written before it can be read by others. Even then, I make mistakes and fail to see that the written words could be misunderstood or taken the wrong way. However, I believe spoken words are even harder to monitor. Once they leave our lips, there is no opportunity to take them back no matter how remorseful and apologetic we may be. Someone has said, "Trying to take back spoken words is like trying to gather up the feathers from a pillow after you have ripped it apart and shaken it in the wind."

The words we use are so important. For example, one lover told his girlfriend under a romantic moon, "Honey, when I look at you, time stands still." Another told his, "Honey, you have a face that would stop a clock." Both young men may have intended to say the same thing, but their choice of words carried a very different message. While this may be an exaggerated illustration, the point is that we need to be aware of the possible impact of the language we use and the need to choose our words wisely.

We are also responsible for the way in which we verbally respond to angry words. It is human nature to react to anger with more of the same. However, we are given insight for the proper response to anger in Proverbs 15:1, *a gentle answer turns away wrath, but a harsh word stirs up anger.*

Suffice it to say that communication is a critical part of our lives and affects every relationship. It behooves us to give serious thought to the impact of our conversation. When we do, there should be no need for gathering feathers in the wind.

Gifts That Keep on Giving

But these are written that you may believe that Jesus is the Christ, the Son of God, and that by believing you may have life in his name.
JOHN 20:31

Occasionally, I get on a binge of decluttering. Usually, it begins with going through paperwork and cards. It almost always ends in my spending several hours reading the collection of cards, reliving each event they represent, then putting them all back into the box. I enjoy email and other modern technology, but I must admit, cards are very special. Perhaps it's because they just keep on giving.

My box of treasures includes letters and notes from a wide spectrum of friends and family who have taken time to write notes from the heart over the years. Each time I read them, it's like reading them for the first time, and a fresh new blessing is attached.

In light of all the technological devices available, it is understandable that the art of handwriting seems to have taken a backseat in schools these days. Still, it makes me sad that students are not having much focus placed on the actual art of cursive writing. How will they come to know the importance of remembering someone with a handwritten note in times of joyous occasions or of illness and grief?

Some of the treasures in my box are letters from my husband, mama, and daddy, now deceased. No amount of typed information could duplicate the feeling of recognizing a loved one's handwriting and knowing it represents their very presence with us. Never underestimate the value of a written note. It may bring joy to someone for many years.

Not to compare our own notes with the inspired Word of God, but I can't help but wonder if the disciples of Jesus, and other writers of the Bible, ever dreamed that the words they wrote would affect people into perpetuity. God's Word is the epitome of a gift that keeps on giving!

Grandparents Are a Different Breed

Children's children are a crown to the aged, and parents are the pride of their children.
PROVERBS 17:6

If you are among those baffled by the behavior of grandparents, maybe I can shed some light on, if not defend, our out-of-character conduct.

My vocabulary does not contain adequate words to express what it's like to be a grandparent. There is no definition sufficient to cover the emotions involved and certainly no logical reasoning for such a sudden change in personality. Therefore, suffice it to say that being a grandparent is one of God's compensations for aging. Here are some of the reasons I believe we change from a rational human being to one of those picture-carrying, bragging zealots that non-grandparents hate to see coming.

It is like we have been given a second chance to see our own children small and cuddly again and are determined to spend more time with them. We have learned to appreciate the little things that children love so much. We have fewer demands on our time and can patiently listen to their requests and make-believe stories. We can send them home when we get tired. We can witness our children deal with some of the same traits in the grands that drove us crazy in them, chuckle under our breath, and know that "this too shall pass." Our faith in God and our experience have a way of lessening the intensity of situations and giving us a longer-range view so that we don't become as flustered about the small stuff as we did when we were younger. This enables us to be less critical and more supportive.

Our vision is altered to the point of missing the children's imperfections and magnifying their beauty, and we wonder why others do not have this same insight. We've learned that one occasional ice cream cone before supper (at our house) will not impair their health for life, and it's all right if they leave a little spinach on their plate occasionally.

Our own children do not recognize us as the same parents that raised them. We admit that we are more lenient now, but that's only because we are confident that our children are raising our grandchildren with the rules and values that they need.

Holding Fast to the Rock

He lifted me out of the slimy pit, out of the mud and mire; he set my feet on a rock and gave me a firm place to stand.
PSALM 40:2

You've heard the old saying, "The only thing certain in life is death and taxes." Contrary to what the world would have us believe, constants do exist that give stability and purpose to those who acknowledge and adhere to them. They are the moral principles upon which our country was founded, as spelled out in God's Word. They were set in motion from the beginning of creation and are as relevant today as the law of gravity. When defied, they are just as devastating.

Our culture would have us believe that watered-down versions or elimination of those principles are appropriate in today's world. Situation ethics are the rule of thumb and heaven forbid that we should take a stand against anything. In the name of tolerance, we are *encouraged* to be silent about our beliefs lest they offend someone. In contrast, language used in movies and television would make a sailor blush, while factions that would take the word God out of public life seem to blush at nothing. Be that as it may, we're prudes if we complain.

Our challenge is to keep God's principles as the guide for our lives. The use of flexible moral principles and gross language in movies and by some of the media have become commonplace. Continual exposure to the *anything goes* morality tends to dull our sensitivity to right and wrong over time without our even realizing it. For example, some of you may remember how shocked we were when Clark Gable said the "d" word in *Gone with the Wind*. Today, if we can find a movie with language as mild as that in *Gone with the Wind*, we're delighted. Things much worse have become routine, and we have almost grown immune to shock.

The bright side of this message is that we do have a rock that can stabilize our world and our lives. When everything around us seems to be falling apart at the seams, God's Word and His principles are our constant that never changes. He stands ready to give us strength, encouragement, and hope for the future if we put our trust in Him.

How Does Adversity Affect You?

"I have told you these things, so that in me you may have peace. In this world you will have trouble. But take heart! I have overcome the world."
JOHN 16:33

Junk e-mail has become as profuse as junk snail mail. Today, however, an anonymous e-mail caught my eye. The gist of it went something like this:

Carol came to her mother with a heart burdened with problems. She confessed that she had become overwhelmed to the point of depression. Without commenting, the mother summoned Carol into the kitchen where she put three pots of water on the stove to boil. Carrots went into one pot, eggs in another, and ground coffee beans into the third. For ten minutes, Carol continued to pour out her heart. As her mother took the pots off the stove, she asked Carol, "What do you see?" "I see carrots, eggs and ground coffee beans," said Carol, "but what's the point?" The mother replied, "They have a lesson to teach us. You see, the carrots, eggs and coffee beans were all faced with the same adversity of hot water, but they all reacted differently. The carrots went in strong and hard, but after a while in the boiling water, became soft and wilted. The egg went into the pot fragile. However, after sitting in the hot water, the thin shell showed no apparent change, although the inside became hardened. Then again the ground coffee beans were different! While they were in the boiling water, they actually changed the water."

"Think about this," the mother continued. "Are you a carrot, an egg, or a coffee bean? The carrots are strong, but wilt and become soft in the face of adversity. The egg starts with a malleable heart, but becomes hardened and stiff with the heat. The eggshell looks the same, but the inside of the egg becomes hardened. In contrast, the coffee beans actually change the water, the very circumstances that cause them pain. When the water gets hot, the coffee beans release their flavor and fragrance, revealing what is inside of them. If you are like the coffee beans, when things are at their worse, you will greatly influence the surrounding circumstances for the better. Those who put their trust in Jesus, by His grace are able to stand and are strengthened through adversity."

This is a simplified analogy, but we might do well to consider our own reaction to hot water.

How Important Are Our Gifts?

Each man should give what he has decided in his heart to give, not reluctantly or under compulsion, for God loves a cheerful giver.
2 CORINTHIANS 9:7

Did you ever consider why God loves a cheerful giver? The Creator of the universe does not need our gifts. He already owns everything. Why, then, does He command us in Malachi 3:10 to bring our tithes and offerings into the storehouse? In the feeding of the five thousand (Matthew 14:13-21), Jesus instructed His disciples to feed the multitude. The only food among the entire group was a lunch offered by one little boy who had five small fishes and two barley loaves. The disciples knew this amount of food was only a drop in the bucket as to the amount needed to feed this vast crowd. Had we been there, we might have said, "Son, keep your bread and fish for yourself. We appreciate your generosity, but it isn't enough to make a difference." But not Jesus! He accepted the boy's gift, blessed it, fed the crowd, and had several baskets of leftovers.

This indicates we don't have to be wealthy to give meaningful gifts to God. What is insignificant to the world may be just what God will use to accomplish His purpose. Our all, plus God, is equal to any task He calls us to do. He does not measure our gifts by the world's standard but by our commitment and love for Him. It was not the size of the lunch but the little boy's willingness to share all he had that thrilled Jesus. By God's awesome power, the gift was sufficient...with leftovers.

If God does not need our gifts, why does He love a cheerful giver? Maybe it's a little like parents who receive gifts from their children. Some may be handprints carefully blotted on a page with crudely scribbled letters of "I love you." Others may be a carefully drawn house with stick people, representing their family, as an expression of their love and adoration. Parents treasure these gifts, not because of their monetary value, but because of the love and meticulous effort children put into them. If parents treasure these kinds of gifts, how much more does God value gifts from His children given with a cheerful and loving heart?

Does that mean, then, that God really does need our gifts? No more than a parent needs a stick figure drawing for the refrigerator or a hug after school, but, oh, how it must thrill His heart!

If You Don't Use It, You Lose It

"Whoever has will be given more, and he will have an abundance. Whoever does not have, even what he has will be taken from him."
MATTHEW 13:12

This verse of scripture may seem mysterious until you realize it refers to understanding God's Word and Jesus's teachings. Then it makes perfect sense. It also makes perfect sense that there may be additional applications for this teaching. One in particular comes to mind—that of use of the mind and body. As time takes its toll on body flexibility, it doesn't take long to learn that the more active we are, the more flexibility and endurance we retain. The same is true of the mind. Doctors tell us that staying active physically and mentally are paramount to good health.

Perhaps that is why retirement does not seem to be on God's agenda for his children. Think about it! Noah was six hundred years of age when the flood came (Genesis 7:6). Abraham was called to move from his homeland at the age of seventy-five and later became the father of a nation (Genesis 12:1-4). Moses was eighty years of age when God called him to return to Egypt to persuade Pharaoh to let his people go (Exodus 7:7).

The moral of this story is simply that God is never finished with us. The more we exercise obedience to His call, the more abilities He gives us to accomplish His purposes. Roles and responsibilities may change. Types of service may be revised. However, God has a plan that is never completed until we go to be with Him. If we look back over our lives carefully, we may be able to see just how each assignment has prepared us for the next.

So...if you have fears that you will outlive your usefulness, don't fret. Stay in touch with the Lord of the universe through prayer and keep your motor running. Your assignments will be exciting. Your mind and body may be limited, but God's power is not!

I'm Sorry

A word aptly spoken is like apples of gold in settings of silver.
PROVERBS 25:11

Nothing sticks in the throat of countless men and women like the words "I'm sorry." It's as if the words, and the humility required, just won't come. Too often, an apology is postponed on the grounds of "Why should I apologize? It wasn't really my fault." Then there is the Hatfield and McCoy approach that says, "I won't have anything to do with that other person, but I don't remember why." There are still people feuding today, even in family circles. I hear people say they have not spoken to a brother, mother, or some other family member in years. That is a classic way to cut off your nose to spite your face. Of course, it takes both parties to reconcile differences, but it only takes one to try.

There are various ways to rationalize or postpone facing the reality that we need to make amends to someone. "I'm sorry" or "I was wrong" are not difficult words to pronounce and don't take much energy to recite.

They don't make your throat swell, but they do require that your ego take a backseat and your pride be replaced with humility. Therein lies the difficulty. Still, it makes no sense to waste time enduring broken relationships when a simple and sincere apology might begin the healing process.

In contrast, children may habitually say "I'm sorry," with little or no feelings of remorse. They learn early the art of circumventing punishment and the rewards of confessing, whether they are sincere or not. Let us pray they will soon learn that words without regret are of little significance.

God was so concerned about broken relationships that He sent His Son to be offered as a sacrifice on our behalf so that our relationship with Him could be reconciled. It was not His place to make the first move; we were the guilty parties. Still, because of His great love for us, Jesus humbled himself and paid our sin debt with his life. Surely, we can muster an apology to others.

If you have trouble saying "I'm sorry," try practicing it in prayer. If you come to God in true repentance, you will experience His forgiveness. Then,

His power will enable you to say those words sincerely to others.

In the Twinkling of an Eye

Many are the plans in a man's heart, but it is the LORD's purpose that prevails.
PROVERBS 19:21

In the twinkling of an eye, Sean's life was changed! His plan to enter college in the fall on a full football scholarship was suddenly shattered by a four-wheeler as it overturned and pinned him underneath. What started out to be a day of excitement ended in painful surgery with a prognosis of possible paralysis in his legs. How quickly his dreams were shattered.

The first thing Sean saw as he slowly aroused from the anesthesia was a bright light above his bed. He could see blurred figures in green as they hovered around him. Whispering voices in the background discussed his surgery and expressed concern for his future. "He has a good chance of survival, but walking, that's another story," said one doctor. "He's lucky to be alive," said another.

Lucky? he thought. Even in his sedated condition, Sean could feel the shock of those words, and they produced numbness of heart and mind. His brain could not process thoughts of never playing football again. His physical pain dimmed in comparison to the ache in his heart. Shattered dreams were all he could envision, dreams he feared might never be put together again. As he drifted back and forth into semi-consciousness, he kept praying to awaken and find he had had a horrible nightmare. As he became more alert, the realization of the event became clearer and the pain more severe.

Space does not permit full details, but Sean did recover and by the following September was able to play football again. By the grace of God and his refusal to give up hope, he was able to rise above his setback and go forward with his dreams.

People fall prey to split-second life-changing experiences every day, and some are not as fortunate as Sean. While we are not in control of many things that come our way, we are in control of how we deal with them. The power and the hope through faith in God's grace is available to all of us.

Is Busyness Your Idol?

The Master said, "Martha, dear Martha, you're fussing far too much and getting yourself worked up over nothing. One thing only is essential, and Mary has chosen it—it's the main course, and won't be taken from her."
Luke 10:41-42 (The Message)

Remembering birthdays of friends and family is an important way to let them know we care. Unfortunately, our tendency is to take things and people for granted. We may make a big deal over someone the world deems "important," but our family and friends, who stand by us every day, may sometimes come up on the short end of the stick with regard to our time and affection.

The busyness of our daily routine can get in the way of things that are most important. Busyness has been described as one of the American idols. As this concept tumbled in my head, I realized it may be an idol of mine! It just may be one of yours as well.

My favorite book gives examples of busyness skewing priorities. One is the familiar encounter between Mary and Martha. Ladies, can't you just see yourself as

Martha, rushing around in the kitchen getting a meal ready for a bunch of hungry men? Of course, Martha wanted to be involved in entertaining the guests, but she was thinking, *Someone has to get this meal ready! There is no way I can stop and visit. Bread is in the oven; the table has to be set. Why isn't Mary helping me?* Then she said to Jesus, "Master, don't you care that my sister has abandoned the kitchen to me? Tell her to lend me a hand" (Luke 10:40 The Message). His reply was not what Martha had expected. Instead, Jesus told her that Mary had made the wiser choice. We are not told how Martha responded, but I like to imagine she removed the bread from the oven and sat down with Mary, realizing the meal could just be late!

Busyness in itself may not be bad. The things we're rushing to do can be good. It's when they deter us from doing the little caring things like hugging a child, *listening* to him or her, stopping to help a hurting friend, making a phone call to a shut-in, or spending time with the Lord that they become a hindrance and may ultimately become an idol.

It's Not My Fault

The man said, "The woman you put here with me—she gave me some fruit from the tree, and I ate it." Then the Lord God said to the woman, "What is this you have done?" The woman said, "The serpent deceived me, and I ate."
GENESIS 3:12-13

Ever wonder why people make excuses? I attribute my inclination to do so to Adam and Eve. Remember? Adam started it all when he blamed Eve for his sin and insinuated that it was God's fault for putting them together. Then Eve followed suit by blaming the serpent. People have continued to find excuses for their behavior ever since. Actually, placing blame is much easier than admitting the truth and accepting responsibility.

Adam and Eve couldn't blame their parents, a broken home, being too rich or too poor, or any of the other social issues that are so often used, so they resorted to blaming others. Today, we have a wider variety of choices, and most of us take full advantage of them.

Children learn early there are excuses for not doing what they are asked to do. Their stomach hurts when you offer them food they don't want to try, and they are tired when it's time to put away toys. "Everyone else is doing it" is just one familiar pretext teens use for following the popular trends of the day. By the time we reach adulthood, we've become proficient in the art of placing blame. It's easy to convince ourselves that obesity is in our genes and our quick temper cannot be controlled. "It's just who I am." There are a zillion other excuses for various shortcomings, but you get the picture.

Why do we do it? Possibilities come to mind. With a lifetime of excuses under our belt, we may have difficulty recognizing truth. If we are confronted with the truth, we are compelled to consider what corrective action is required, and the ball is in our court. In reality, while we are creating excuses, we could be setting sails toward a better future.

It's misguided to presume that circumstances, traits, and other people don't affect our lives, but none of these have to have the final say. The Holy Spirit is in our corner, whispering words of encouragement and making

His power available to us. His way is not easy, but it is the way of truth. It is the way of victory over excuses and of taking responsibility for our actions.

Joy of Ordinary Days

This is the day the LORD has made; let us rejoice and be glad in it.
PSALM 118:24

I'm not quite sure how or when it began, but I have come to treasure *ordinary* days. These are days when there is nothing specific on my agenda and no crisis in the country or among family or friends. They are days when there are no scheduled meetings, appointments, or things that must be done today. There is time for an extra cup of coffee, a casual phone call, and an extra moment for meditation, scanning junk mail, playing catch-up on neglected chores, and renewing of my mind and soul. Even when days begin as ordinary, they sometimes change in the twinkling of an eye. Ones that don't change are few and far between. Perhaps that's why they are so special and are to be treasured.

For the worrier, the absence of a crisis allows more time to conjure up trivia about which to be concerned. The adventurer might experience boredom in the absence of excitement. The pragmatist might feel guilty for not seeming to accomplish something worthwhile. However, for believers, every new day is a day that the Lord has made, and we have every reason to rejoice and be glad. We can trust Him to take care of our worries, so we can check that one off. As for boredom, what could be more exciting than communing with the Lord of the universe? Also, believers need never feel guilty for spending an ordinary day enjoying God's beautiful world and basking in His presence. It is on days like these that our bodies, minds, and souls are refreshed, replenished, and restored.

Regardless of what's on your agenda for today, try to find a reason to be thankful, rejoice, and be glad.

Laughter is Good Medicine

A cheerful heart is good medicine, but a crushed spirit dries up the bones.
PROVERBS 17:22

If laughter is good medicine, I should be healthy to the bone. The choice is mine. I can either laugh at myself or be miserable wondering what is happening to my mind and body. When my brain won't pull up the answer to a simple question about someone's name, it's much easier to ask, "How soon do you need to know?" than to become frustrated and embarrassed.

Laughter really is relaxing, and many doctors believe it has medicinal value. Research is unclear because there are so many factors involved, but one thing is certain. When you're laughing, even at yourself, you can't be fretting at the same time.

There is some comfort in knowing that all forgetfulness is not limited to the aging process. Recently, I saw a lady frantically looking for her umbrella that was hanging on her arm, and she was not old by any stretch. The two items most often lost at my house are cordless phones and television remotes. If you ever call me and I don't answer before the answering machine comes on, it may mean I'm out of town. More likely than not, however, it means I'm at home looking for the telephone.

As years have gone by and my lifestyle has become less stressful, my forgetfulness has not improved much, but the way I deal with it has! It's OK for older people to forget. We have earned the right, and we soon forget what we forgot so it must not have been so important anyway. Besides, it is comforting to know that smarter people than I struggle with some of these same experiences.

On a more serious note, we can do things to help our memory. Getting plenty of rest, writing things down, ridding ourselves of busy things that don't matter, setting aside quiet time, and exercising are just a few. You can ask God to calm your heart and soul and fill you with His peace and power. You can pause and do this anywhere. Believe it or not, He is interested in every detail of your life and will help find the car keys as well as deal with major crises.

Don't be afraid to laugh at yourself. Laughter really is good medicine!

When Life Tosses You a Lemon, Make Lemonade

Dear friends, now we are children of God, and what we will be has not yet been made known. But we know that when he appears, we shall be like him, for we shall see him as he is.
1 JOHN 3:2

One of the great mysteries of life is why some people use obstacles as opportunities, and others use them as excuses. There are those who retreat and "sour away" when life throws them a lemon while others make lemonade and continue to live life to the fullest.

It's true that life doesn't always seem fair, but sooner or later, everyone will have adversities. The Bible tells us that. It's part of life and our maturing process. We are not told why every person is not given the same number of talents, but we are told that we are responsible for using the ones we have to the best of our ability and for the glory of God.

God is under no more of an obligation to explain why He makes us different from one another than a potter is to explain why he makes one pot to be used for food and the next for decoration. It should be sufficient to know that we are His work in progress.

I am often reminded through television ads of the disabilities of our men and women in the military who have been wounded while serving our country. We see loss of limbs, loss of sight, and severe burns, just to name a few. In most cases, we find that these young men and women continue their fight through recovery and rehabilitation with the same resolve they had in battle. What an inspiration they are to those of us who may complain about stiff knees and arthritis when they are going strong with no knees or with other disabling amputations. Their spirit of survival is contagious and should inspire all of us to start squeezing the lemons instead of soaking in our sour state.

Whatever our lot, we can be encouraged by the fact that our earthly tenure is but a twinkling of an eye in comparison to the time we will have to enjoy our new body with perfect health and peace with our Lord in eternity.

Living in the Shadow of Fear

There is no fear in love. But perfect love drives out fear, because fear has to do with punishment. The one who fears is not made perfect in love.
1 JOHN 4:18

Numerous articles and quotations have been written about dealing with fear. Everyone has had some experience with this emotion. Paul recognized fear as being a deterrent for service as he wrote to Timothy, "For God has not given us a spirit of fear, but of power and of love and of a sound mind" (2 Timothy 1:7 New King James Version).

Franklin D. Roosevelt once said, "…the only thing we have to fear is fear itself.…" I was certain this statement pertained to World War II. Actually, it was part of his first inaugural address on March 4, 1933, in the midst of the Great Depression. There was fear then about the financial future of our country.

From the time we are born until we die, we face uncertainties and unknowns of all kinds that may cause us to fear. Children may fear the dark. Later they may fear not being accepted by peers. Then come the adult years and there are still more uncertainties. Will my marriage work? Will I get the promotion? How susceptible am I to cancer, heart disease, etc.? Will my children be successful?

Fear can result in paralysis that may cause a person or a nation to refrain from action of any kind. In this case, the enemy wins without a fight. Fear can also cause people to become timid and withdrawn when boldness and confidence are required for endurance.

Satan used fear to render Peter ineffective on the night that Jesus was arrested (John 18:25-27). Yet through the power of the Holy Spirit, some fifty days later, Peter stood up and spoke with boldness and conviction before thousands of unbelievers (Acts 2:14-36).

In God's Word we have been given the tools for strengthening our faith and dispelling fear. A great way to stay focused and keep our lives in perspective is to read and claim His promises for deliverance. They can help to free us from alarm as we live in the very shadow of fear.

Need a Memory Pill?

He makes me lie down in green pastures, he leads me beside quiet waters, he restores my soul. He guides me in paths of righteousness for his name's sake.
PSALM 23:2-3

With all the research and discovery taking place in the medical field today, why hasn't someone concocted a memory pill? I'm serious! There may be some medications that will help to improve memory for certain diseases, but I mean a pill just for the scatterbrain who still makes lists and forgets to read them. Technology has developed methods to relieve computer overload by defragging or adding memory but nothing to enhance or defrag our own memory.

Come to think of it, remembering may be worse than forgetting. There are those who have trouble letting go of things and carry grudges for years. What a waste of time and energy. Many things, like resentment, need to be forgotten. It's a shame we can't categorize events as they occur into *remember* and *forget* files and process them accordingly. If that were a successful process, it would eliminate our continual beating ourselves over the head for mistakes and sins that God has long forgiven and forgotten.

The psalmist praises God in Psalm 139:14 saying, "I praise you because I am fearfully and wonderfully made; your works are wonderful, I know that full well." That being the case, we can be assured that God has made provisions for restoration and defragging of all of us through fervent prayer and Bible study. His Word is filled with instructions on how to be renewed and refreshed. If we can learn to let Him be in charge and handle the anxiety, we will have more time to relax and remember those instructions we have been given.

I praise God for wonderful memories and even more for things I am able to forget. Most of all, I praise Him for His mercy, forgiveness of sin, and His promises of restoration, peace, and love.

Music, the Universal Language

Speak to one another with psalms, hymns and spiritual songs. Sing and make music in your heart to the Lord...
EPHESIANS 5:19

The wonder of music and the influence it has on people is one of life's mysteries. As a music lover, the classics and big band era music are some of my favorites, and each familiar tune brings back a certain memory of a special event, friend, or unique experience. It's exciting to hear ones that were long forgotten and yet were such an important part of the past. The complex brain that God has placed inside our heads has a way of pulling up closed files just by the sound of a familiar song. Some bring joy and others pain, but all are incredibly real.

Music is a universal language, one that everyone can understand and appreciate. It inspires, motivates, uplifts, and even gives energy. It helps to use music when you are walking to give rhythm and spring to your step. In fact, people in the military will tell you when they think they have tramped their last mile, a military band can strike up a lively march, and it brings them new energy and a second wind. How can that be? What mystical influence does music have upon our bodies and our minds?

When one of my granddaughters was nine months old, she had meningitis and was in a coma for five days. The doctor gave us no hope of recovery. He did say it might help if we put her favorite musical toy in her bed. He thought perhaps she could hear, and familiar music might come through to her. Many prayers were going up on her behalf and miraculously, she survived and is perfectly normal. We will never know what part, if any, the music played in her recovery, but one thing is sure, it was worth a try. Of course, we know her healing came from God, however He chose to do it.

It's exciting to know that God loves and communicates through music, and we can be sure that heaven will be filled with sounds more beautiful than we can imagine.

Relinquishing Control

As obedient children, do not conform to the evil desires you had when you lived in ignorance.
1 PETER 1:14

Nothing exemplifies the power of God more than that of a changed life. It was obvious to me, as I talked with an old friend, that something was very different about him. There was a new gleam in his eye and a redirection of the tremendous amount of energy that has characterized his life. It was as if he were on automatic pilot, not really understanding the power that was driving him. His gear seemed to be in neutral with God at the wheel. It blessed my soul to see God at work in such a mighty way.

Why doesn't every believer have that same glow? Could it depend upon the degree of commitment or willingness to let God lead? I believe there is something compelling in each of us that makes us want to remain in control.

For many years, my husband was not content in a car unless he was driving. It was not until he became ill that he realized how much more he could see and appreciate without having to watch the road. He actually learned to relax and enjoy the ride.

Many of us are like this with regard to our daily lives. We commit ourselves to the Lord and accept His forgiveness, yet we hesitate to give Him complete control of the wheel on a daily basis. The times I've been able to relinquish the driver's seat have been peaceful and rewarding. When God is in control, there is no worry about taking a wrong turn or getting sidetracked. There is no need for concern about arriving at our destination on time because His timing is perfect and His direction is sure.

Knowing that God's will is best and His power is immeasurable, why then is it so hard to give up our control? Maybe it's a lack of trust. We've been driving all these years and never had an accident! Well, maybe a few scrapes, but it feels so safe to have our hands on the wheel. That is, until we find ourselves stuck in the mud and need a push or a pull.

"O God, grant us the wisdom to know how much we need your guidance before we get stuck."

Sanding the Rough Edges

If it is possible, as far as it depends on you, live at peace with everyone.
ROMANS 12:18

God never ceases to amaze me in the way He uses people to accomplish His purpose in each of us. Do you have individuals in your life who seem to exist for the sole purpose of rubbing you the wrong way? If you don't, you're likely the exception rather than the rule. But have you considered that maybe God sends them into our lives to sand off our own rough edges? If that's the case, some of us must have more rough edges than others. In any event, abrasive or brutally frank people definitely provide us with opportunities to improve our character.

Our challenge is to live at peace with everyone, if it is possible, as stated in the scripture above. It becomes easier, however, if we can realize that even the "hard-to-deal-with folks" can add value to our lives. It also helps to understand that this life is our basic training for eternity. Just as the military uses very stringent training techniques to enable our military men and women to achieve maximum readiness for battle, God uses rigorous and sometimes severe training in order to mold us into His image.

We may not be called upon to perform one hundred push-ups at five o'clock in the morning, but the muscles of our patience may be flexed to the limit in dealing with an obnoxious friend or family member.

God, in His infinite wisdom, has chosen to bring us into the physical world as helpless babies. We are nurtured and fed by parents until we have reached independent status. He has also chosen to bring us into His family as babes in Christ, needing spiritual nurturing, food, and sometimes, serious sanding.

The next time someone rubs you the wrong way, try and view the occurrence from a different perspective. Consider what you can learn from the clash, then pray for the other person. Be instrumental in making this sandpaper moment constructive for both of you.

Seasons of Change

There is a time for everything, and a season for every activity under heaven: ...a time to keep and a time to throw away.
ECCLESIASTES 3:1, 6B

In the process of moving in recent years, a lot of things were discarded that I would never have considered discarding a few years earlier. It's amazing how many "things" we accumulate. It is also amazing how the attachment fades after you have packed and unpacked them. As I parted with sentimental items one by one, this passage from Ecclesiastes rang loudly in my ears. Not only had the season of my life changed, but my priorities had as well. Instead of asking myself "Will I regret it if I let this go?", my question became "How meaningful will this be to my children?" The answer to that question changed my perspective entirely, and the decision making became a breeze. The clutter has been eliminated, but I can already tell that the "throw away" season will need to come again soon.

Speaking of seasons, I totally missed the autumn of my life. I guess I always related autumn with being "middle-aged," and by the time I was ready to admit to being middle-aged, the snowstorms of winter had already begun. Forty or even fifty just seemed too young to be called "middle-aged," and so I rationalized myself right through that era to the dead of winter. Come to think of it, winter has always been my very favorite season!

Life's winter season has many benefits. It takes longer to get things done, but the deadlines are less stringent. The intensity of life has mellowed, but appreciation of little things has become more intense. The earth seems more beautiful, the birds sing with more gusto, and family and friends are more revered and cherished.

In the midst of the aches and pains of winter, I am deeply aware of the brevity of life. I do not need to be reminded that every day is priceless, and I am challenged to live each moment to the fullest, embracing the change!

Seeing is Believing—Or Is It?

"Therefore I speak to them in parables; because seeing, they do not see, and hearing they do not hear, nor do they understand."
MATTHEW 13:13 (NKJV)

Recently, an excited friend could hardly wait to tell me about her cataract surgery. She raved that the procedure had improved her television clarity so much that she has cancelled plans to replace her TV set. Now that she has 20/20 vision, she can readily understand that her vision problems were her own eyes rather than the objects around her.

Have you ever really considered what part your vision plays in your daily life? Eyes reveal to the brain what things look like. Seeing is believing, isn't it? Reflect for a moment about this lady. She truly believed what she saw, but she was wrong! She was actually seeing the world through a film that dimmed objects not in keeping with actuality. She was not able to see things as they really are until the miracle of surgery took place.

If bodily vision is crucial to our well-being, what about our spiritual vision? It, too, can become clouded by diseases of sin in the form of selfishness, pride, ambition, greed, apathy, or just plain laziness. Spiritual blindness is not a self-help condition any more than correcting our own cataracts would be. But the skilled hands of our Creator Physician have the ability to remove the obstacles that blind us. He can give us a clear vision of the world as it really is. He requires only that we put our faith and trust in Him and repent of our sins. The procedure is free. The enormous expense has been paid in advance by Him who loves us with an immeasurable love. After this spiritual surgery—or new birth—colors become more vivid, people more beautiful, needs more apparent, and our hearts more loving as the implants of Jesus Christ Himself filter our vision. Then and only then does our spiritual vision become 20/20. With the light of His Spirit to guide us, hope is renewed and trust restored. Fear is no longer a dominant force because the Light of the World wipes away the dark corners and sinful shadows. What a difference clear vision makes!

It is a terrible thing to see and have no vision.
HELEN KELLER

Sitting on the Fence

...But as for me and my household, we will serve the Lord.
JOSHUA 24:15

The stance of indecision has stunned me many times over the years. The reality that men and women held in high esteem, in roles of authority and influence, can be reluctant to take a stand on important issues was one of my *real world* rude awakenings. In most instances, "sitting on the fence" is a negative. Sitting on the fence is an indecisive stance chosen most often to circumvent criticism or conflict.

You may have heard it said of people that they are "sitting on the fence, ready to fall either way." This is another way of saying they are waiting for enough information to determine the outcome and will take sides with the winner, once that outcome is known. There are many fence occupants.

How many people do you know who are willing to be the first to stand up for an issue even when it's not a popular one? How many fall into the group of waiting for others to commit to something and then following suit when it looks like a majority situation. It takes courage to be a leader, but the comfort zone of many of us dictates caution at best and sitting on the fence in more difficult situations. There is nothing wrong with waiting to get sufficient facts to make intelligent decisions, but the fear of criticism can cause the faint-hearted to fall prey to peer pressure.

There are many situations in which Christians need to exercise tolerance. Paul writes in Romans 12:18, "If it is possible, as far as it depends on you, live at peace with everyone." However, John quotes Jesus as saying in Revelation 3:16, "So, because you are lukewarm—neither hot nor cold—I am about to spit you out of my mouth."

Our country is a melting pot of many cultures that brings with it the temptation to compromise beliefs. I believe the time has come when survival of our values is at stake. How many waves are we willing to make to turn the tide from "anything goes" to standards of decency? Our future depends on our getting off the fence and letting our voices be heard. Remember, Satan owns the fence.

Squandering Your Inheritance

Jesus continued: "There was a man with two sons. The younger one said to his father, 'Father, give me my share of the estate.' So he divided his property between them. . . . After he had spent everything, there was a severe famine in that whole country, and he began to be in need."
LUKE 15:11-12, 14

The story of the Prodigal Son has always been one of my favorite parables in the Bible. There are so many personalities and points of view to explore. As with all scripture, every time you read it, God may reveal a different message from it just for you.

As was the case in this parable, inheritance is generally thought of as property, money, or some other financial asset. With age, however, material things tend to become less important—at least for me—and things of lasting value become more precious. In that light, let's think about our inheritance that money cannot and did not buy.

Most of us were given a reasonable measure of good health, a sound mind, talents in varying number, opportunities, freedom of choice, and so on. One gift that gains added appreciation as years go by is good health. How can we squander good health? Let me count the ways: (1) overeating, (2) lack of exercise, (3) smoking, (4) drug and alcohol abuse, (5) pursuing financial and career goals at the expense of our health. I'm sure there are many others.

All of the above are old hat and general knowledge to most people. Maybe it is because they are old hat that we have come to ignore the warning signs of our bodies and advice from our doctors. Good health is such a treasure, one that we should work to preserve.

How can it be, that in this world of mind-boggling medical technology and advanced medicine, we tend to neglect what we know to be vital to our well-being? Let me challenge you to take time to inventory your inheritance items that money cannot buy. Chances are, you will find that you are richer than you thought. While you're at it, think of ways you need to be taking care of and using those priceless gifts for your good, as well as the good of others, and to the glory of God.

Teach Them to Love

Her children arise and call her blessed...
PROVERBS 31:28

A young mother recently posed the question to me, "If you could tell me one thing that we should teach our children in order to have them respect their parents when they grow up, what would it be?" This question caught me off guard and left me speechless for a moment. While I was thinking, *Why are you asking me, I am no expert*, I uttered the first thing that came to mind, "Teach them how to love." Her question kept the wheels turning in my head for several days and caused me to recall my own parents and pleasant childhood days. It also caused me to question my answer and to delve deeper into the subject.

Things that stand out about my own parents were their unquestionable love of God and their unconditional love and sacrifices for their children. They taught us by example, as well as verbally, the importance of loving God and loving one another. This love was not dependent upon whether we were on the honor roll every month, but it certainly inspired me to study more. It was not dependent upon our looks, talent, or popularity. We were their children, they loved us, and we knew they always would.

Certainly, there are many educated answers to this question. However, I could not help thinking about the teenagers who have been involved in school shootings, bullying, and other crimes at such an early age and wondering how much love they had experienced in their own lives.

After having had time to ponder this question, my answer is still the same, with one important note. The perfect example of unconditional love is Jesus Christ. In Romans 5:8, we read, "But God demonstrates his own love for us in this: While we were still sinners, Christ died for us." I believe that if we can relay this message to our children by example, the respect will naturally come.

Let us say a prayer for the parents who face teaching their young children to show respect and honor in today's world, where it is not popular or cool to do so.

The Gift of Life

"But seek first his kingdom and his righteousness, and all these things will be given to you as well."
MATTHEW 6:33

The old adage, "I have more time than I have money," may not be a realistic way to look at life. For one thing, there is always the possibility of earning more money, but no one has the ability to add one second to our life span. Granted, we may work toward extending our lives by eating right and exercising. Surely, that is important. However, only God knows His plan for us and, ultimately, our life span is in His hands.

With that in mind, wouldn't you agree that time is our most valuable asset? In fact, I believe it falls into the category of priceless. In contrast, however, we tend to put more thought and time into budgeting and investing our money than we do determining how to invest our time wisely.

I am not suggesting that we use a scheduler for every minute of the day based on the *time is money* philosophy. What I am saying is that using our time wisely is at least of equal importance as being a good steward of our worldly goods. Since time is actually life itself, we can expect to be held accountable for the use of it. Someone has aptly stated, "Time waits for no man." The opportunities of each day may never come our way again. Children and grandchildren grow up so quickly and people die unexpectedly. Situations change daily and it behooves us to take advantage of every opportunity. Our "to do" list may not include building lasting relationships, lending a helping hand to those in need, or listening to God's still voice. But if it doesn't, we are missing the very purpose of life itself. When we can look at our lives through the eyes of God and grasp that we were created to live for eternity, everything takes on a new dimension. It puts our priorities and our daily schedule in a whole new light.

The Other Side of the Mountain

Enter his gates with thanksgiving and his courts with praise; give thanks to him and praise his name. For the LORD is good and his love endures forever; his faithfulness continues through all generations.
PSALM 100:4-5

On my first visit to the Pacific Northwest, the height of the trees blew me away. The beauty of the area was breathtaking, but I was mesmerized by the height of the trees. They were so much taller than we usually see in the Southeast, it was awesome. My favorites were the firs and spruce that we seldom see, except at Christmas.

These phenomenal trees came to mind again when we had visitors from the Dallas, Texas, area. Their teenage daughter, who had never visited this part of the country, kept referring to the "tall green trees" here. I was confused at first, until I remembered how few and how short the trees near Dallas are. How ironic that I was quick to sell short our own scenery by comparing trees in Georgia to Washington State, but when comparing Georgia to Texas, our trees really are tall. The old saying about the grass always being greener on the other side of the mountain took on new meaning for me. It became clear once again, that what one person takes for granted as ordinary, another might see as remarkable. Sometimes it takes new eyes and a fresh look to remind us of the blessings at our doorsteps.

Whether our trees are short or tall, sparse or dense, God's blessings abound wherever we are. His goodness is evident in all the earth. Our challenge is to be conscious of each blessing and to respond to God with thanksgiving and praise. Please pray with me for eyes to see the beauty on our side of the mountain and for thankful hearts to God for His goodness, faithfulness, and enduring love.

The Power of the Tongue

The tongue that brings healing is a tree of life, but a deceitful tongue crushes the spirit.
PROVERBS 15:4

In an era when gun control is a big issue, it seems fitting to consider another dangerous weapon—the tongue! It is accessible to everyone with a voice and may have the ability to cause more pain than a gun or knife.

We wouldn't dare hand a small child a loaded gun, yet we may fail to teach him to use restraint and respect when speaking to others. We even excuse our own outbursts by confessing that "what comes up comes out. That's just who I am." That is not very comforting if you happen to be on the receiving end of an outburst. Perhaps we have become so caught up in our right of "freedom of speech," we have lost sight of the responsibilities attached. All things that are legal aren't necessarily advisable.

Have you ever stopped to consider just how powerful your own tongue can be? Just for starters, you have the ability to console, to comfort, to express love, to encourage, to build up, and to praise. Still, with that same tongue, you can spew out vulgarity, profanity, discouragement, destroy a reputation, kill incentive, thwart character growth, and impede justice. If you think your words don't matter, ask a family member or friend.

Someone has said that when we are bumped, the contents of our inner being spill out. If that be true, anger, contempt, and hostility have set up housekeeping in many hearts and minds. There are countless evils in the world over which we have no control, but this is not true of our tongues. It may take some habit changes, repentance, and prayer, but with the help of God, we can control our tongues.

In this communication age, it is frightening to consider that through the Internet and other media, almost everyone has the ability to be heard worldwide. Let us join together in prayer that we will always communicate in a spirit of truth and love with the purpose to accomplish good.

A closed mouth gathers no foot.
Author unknown

Time Is a Very Special Gift

...For what is your life? It is even a vapor that appears for a little time and then vanishes away.
JAMES 4:14 (NKJV)

God gives us many gifts we tend to take for granted, not the least of which is time. Even though the length of our lives varies from one extreme to the other every day we live consists of 24 hours. This is a constant, regardless of wealth, age, or status. We cannot buy, sell, save, hoard, stretch, or give time away. Yet, how we use it determines our future.

Some people spend time worrying about tomorrow, making today unproductive. Worry may be the biggest thief of time we face. It saps energy, wastes time, and, taken to the extreme, renders us totally ineffective. It accomplishes nothing except to obstruct our appreciation of and joy in life in the present. Worry grieves God because He wants us to trust Him to take care of tomorrow.

Others spend a lifetime living for tomorrow. It may be in the form of saving for retirement, planning for children's and grandchildren's futures, building a dream house, or acquiring property or other "things." These are not bad in themselves unless they consume your time to the point of missing the joys of today. We are not promised tomorrow so to become totally engrossed in planning the future is not wise. (See Luke 12:20)

Still others live by the motto of "Eat, drink, and be merry for tomorrow you may die." One with this view wastes time and finds no purpose or fulfillment in the folly that he has chosen.

How then should we spend our time? God has a different plan for each of us, but there are guidelines that fit all. Pray for wisdom and guidance, give thanks for and enjoy the blessings of every day, trust in God to take care of tomorrow, and be obedient to His call. We have been given the instructions and the power, the rest is up to us! Every day is a special gift, and we dare not waste it foolishly.

What Difference Can One Person Make?

But Jonah ran away from the LORD and headed for Tarshish. He went down to Joppa, where he found a ship bound for that port. After paying the fare, he went aboard and sailed for Tarshish to flee from the LORD.

JONAH 1:3

In a spectator society, it is much less stressful to stand on the sidelines of life and cheer or criticize the players than become involved with the action. Ruts become very comfortable, and it is easy to be lulled to sleep by complacency, especially if you convince yourself that one person can do very little to change things anyway.

The story of Jonah reminds me to what extent one may be willing to go to avoid affecting change, especially if it is something he really doesn't want to do. You remember Jonah. He made the mistake of thinking he could run away from God, and God used a big fish to get his attention. Then, as he followed God's instructions, he was able to make a difference, and the whole city of Nineveh was spared.

Everyone does not experience a dramatic encounter like Jonah did, but we are confronted with worldly issues and decisions that challenge our values and faith. It takes some intestinal fortitude to take a right stand when it is not the politically correct or popular position, but it is important that we stand for the right thing anyway. As Edmund Burke said, "All that is necessary for evil to flourish is for good men to do nothing." Tolerance can be a virtue until it collides with God's moral law. Sometimes, all it takes for a tidal wave of godliness to begin is for one brave person to dare to speak out. Timidity melts in the presence of courage.

What can one person do? You may never know. God can use the smallest deed to accomplish much. I am reminded of the widow's offering in Luke 21:2-4. Even though her contribution was only two small coins, Luke tells us it was all she had. Little did she know that her faithfulness in giving would inspire people for centuries to come. Our duty is to stand firm in truth and be obedient to God's call. He can use our efforts to accomplish more than we can imagine.

When All Else Fails, Read the Instructions

Your word is a lamp to my feet and a light for my path.
PSALM 119:105

How many times have you bought something you weren't quite sure how to operate? It could be something as small as a can opener to something as complex as a computer or as expensive as an automobile. In any case, the item probably came with an owner's manual. The manufacturer normally starts with the safety features and then includes operator instructions, maintenance instructions, and troubleshooting tips.

The intent of operator manuals is to insure that the item is properly used for maximum performance and customer satisfaction. We all know that, right? Yet more times than I want to count, I have plunged into a project without looking at the instructions and then became totally distraught from trying it my way. When all else failed, I'd read the instructions. Does this sound familiar? Wasting time and sometimes destroying the product has given me a new appreciation for instructions.

God, in His infinite wisdom, has given us a comprehensive manual for living. It begins with Genesis and ends with Revelation. In these books you will find safety features (how to be saved and live according to God's purpose), operator instructions (how to live in relationship to God and others), maintenance instructions (how to grow in faithfulness and love), and troubleshooting tips (what to do in times of trouble). Most of us are familiar with this Holy Book. Yet, many times we are guilty of leaving our Creator out of decisions or failing to read the instructions that would help us avoid pitfalls and heartache.

God's Word lights our way in a dark world, provides encouragement when we're down, strengthens us when we are weak, assures us of God's love and presence when we feel alone, and guides us home when we've lost our way. This should be sufficient incentive for us to read the instructions *before* all else fails!

Why Pray?

For the eyes of the Lord are on the righteous and his ears are attentive to their prayer...
1 PETER 3:12

If God knows our every thought and need—and He does—why do you suppose Jesus prayed and set the example for us? If it was necessary for Jesus to pray, surely we need it more. No one can fully understand the heart of God but, as a parent, I can recognize some similarity of having my children bring requests to me. Even when they asked for things not in their best interest, the fact that they asked gave us a chance to discuss the issue and talk it through. In most cases, we could reach an agreement after having considered each other's perspective.

Since God has an overall plan for the future and sees what is ahead, He knows what is best. He also longs to have a close relationship with his children that only comes from spending time in prayer in a two-way conversation. In fact, maybe we need to spend more time listening than we do talking. It's beyond explanation, but in that communion process, God enlightens our minds and hearts in a way that melts our stubborn will and causes a spirit of submission to fill us, accepting that His will is perfect.

If we find our prayers being answered with "no," we can find comfort in remembering that Jesus also prayed for deliverance from the cross like this: *"Abba, Father,"* he said, *"everything is possible for you. Take this cup from me. Yet not what I will, but what you will"* (Mark 14:36). Through submission to God's will, He was victorious over death, and the plan of salvation for all mankind was made complete.

Prayer is not just an audience with God in which we present our "wish" list. Rather, it is a time of thanksgiving, confession, communion, and submission to God's perfect will, allowing Him to renew our minds and hearts and continue his work of molding us into the very image of Christ.

Your Beans Always Come Up

Do not be deceived: God cannot be mocked. A man reaps what he sows.
GALATIANS 6:7

Jason's father was planting his garden. He assigned Jason the chore of planting three rows of beans. His father prepared the rows and instructed Jason to plant the seed twelve inches apart with three seeds in each hill. He demonstrated how to plant and cover the seeds to be sure Jason understood the procedure.

When Jason had the hang of it, his father left him to finish the job. It was a Saturday and Jason's friends were already gathering for the baseball game. The sun was getting hot and the rows looked a mile long. Grudgingly, Jason dropped three beans, covered them lightly, and twelve inches further he dropped three more. As he reached the end of his first row, he had an idea of how to speed things up. He increased the beans from three to six. He suddenly realized that doubling the seeds would cause him to run out of beans before he ran out of rows, so he decided to plant them every two feet instead of one.

As the sun grew hotter, the hills became wider apart until finally Jason decided it was time to wrap it up. He poured the remaining beans into one pile, covered them lightly, reported to his father, and went away to play.

Two weeks later, when Jason got home from school, his father was waiting for him. "Son," he said, "I have something to show you." Jason's heart came up in his throat as they headed for the garden and straight to the beans. There in full view stood one row of beans that looked just right. Next were rows with too many plants in one bunch and long spaces with nothing. The biggest embarrassment was in the last row. There in the middle were dozens of tiny plants huddled together in one big clump. Jason grew pale as he looked up into his father's face. He could see disappointment, but what his father said was a calm statement of truth that stayed with him throughout his life. He simply said, "Son, your beans will always come up!"

Some semblance of this story was told years ago by an inspirational speaker, whose name escapes me, but demonstrates well the law of the harvest. This law is spelled out in Galatians 6:7: "A man reaps what he sows."